Illusion of a Woman

A. M. Thomas

Presentation by *BookLeaf Publishing*

Web: www.bookleafpub.com

E-mail: info@bookleafpub.com

ISBN: 9789357748452

First edition 2023

For Gram, who was one of my first inspirations to write. I will always be your sweetheart.

For Papa, whose sense of humor I may have inherited among other things. I hope you would be proud of the person I've become.

ACKNOWLEDGEMENT

To my husband, Alex - without your encouragement and support, I never would have decided to chase my dreams of becoming published. I love you.

To my sibling, Sam - without you, I simply wouldn't be the person I am today. I love you, thank you for all that you've done and continue to do for me.

To my soul sister, Mariyah - thank you for being a constant during the most tumultuous time in my life. I love you.

To my bestie, Siri - thank you for pushing me beyond my comfort zone in the best ways, and for your support as I navigate life's adventures. I love you.

To my mentor, Professor Kathryn Kysar - your support and guidance during my time at Anoka-Ramsey has meant more than I could ever express. Even now, I still find your lessons to be incredibly valuable and I will hold on to them for the rest of my days. Thank you endlessly.

PREFACE

This poetry collection is a culmination of nearly a decade of creative writing. During my time at Anoka-Ramsey Community College, I took several poetry workshops and other classes to perfect my craft. My mentor, Professor Kathryn Kysar, worked tirelessly with me to compile a manuscript of my best work. The majority of those poems are presented here, along with some newer works of which I am particularly proud.

Many of the poems in Illusions of a Woman are deeply personal, but I feel the need to share them with the world. I hope that by baring my soul on these pages I will inspire others in some way. I am extremely grateful to have had the opportunity to take part in BookLeaf Publishing's #TheWriteAngle Challenge.

Unplug

The ice-cold winds bring snow, completing
the wintery landscape. Joy and misery
are wrapped in the same white silence
that I desperately thaw from within.
/
I find time for solitude and inspiration;
there is time to let the amalgamation
of words in my mind flow out
onto the canvas in front of me.
/
I must concentrate to escape
the distractions of day-to-day life.
I put down my phone, unplug from
my devices and put pen to paper.

Unspoiled Innocence

Tiny fingers, tiny hands
wrapped in the softest blanket
kept warm by mother's arms -
there is nowhere else but here
in this moment
with this new life -
a life completely open to possibility
and chance; a destiny yet unwritten.

There is no love
like the love of an innocent -
pure, unadulterated, unconditional,
fantastic love -
with no prejudice or hate to spoil it.

Hanged

Lurking, stalking,
quietly waiting
for the opportune moment
to strike,

strands of fear and doubt
wisp in the wind,
like the light branches
of a willow tree.

Weaving
doubt and fear
the strands create
a thick rope.

The grip
of anxiety tightens
like a noose
around my neck.

Panicked breathing,
in -- and -- out.
Count to ten, nine, eight,
seven, breathe again, slow.

Prayer for Humanity

Tonight is for the silent,
for the abused and the unheard.
> You may not speak,
> but we will speak for you.

Tonight is for those who are trapped
by something or someone.
> You may not be free,
> but we will free you.

To those who are lost and broken,
may you find your way and be whole again.

To those who leave words unspoken,
may your voice find the courage to return.

To those without food or a bed to sleep in,
may you find help from a willing soul.

To those who are victimized,
may you find the strength to begin anew.

Tonight is for humanity,
for all of those who may find themselves
> silent,
> trapped,
> lost and broken,
> victimized.

May you find a friend, a loving hand to guide you.

Losing You Twice

Like bits of white dandelion fluff
blown from their stem by a child in the summer,
swirling and darting through invisible currents.
you were gone – vanished

like a balloon tied to ribbon,
ripped from a small child's hand
though they gripped it with all their might.
Before I could say goodbye,

we watched as you were buried
not in the ground, but in emptiness
and nothing – your world was filled
with jumbled memories and hollowed moments.

I'm here.

Days and weeks and months
went by, and I was "too busy"
with life to make time to see you.
Until that Thursday in March

when my phone rang
and they told me it was time.
We said goodbye with stories
of your jokes and happy moments

and held your hand as you died
surrounded by those who loved you most.
We will gather in tears and laughter
to remember who you were.

I'm here; I'm still here.

Never Enough

Springtime lilacs bloom
under lovely sunshine and
now I'm missing you.

A week's gone by –
not flown, but dug its heels in
and fought tooth and nail.
Time passes slowly.
What a bitch time is.
There seems to be so much time
when everything is fine,
but the minute things go wrong
there's never enough.

H.P.J.

"my hero"
1938-2006-2017

 Memory [mem'o-ri]: n, the power of retaining and
reproducing mental or sensory impressions; an impression
so reproduced; a having or keeping in the mind; time within
which past things can be remembered…

Nothing can be said to erase
the treasured memories I have
with you—card games and bonfires,
crosswords and "Blackberry ass, all clear!"

I look at you and see pale, frail
skin; weathered hands clutch cold
metal and your eyes refuse to shine.
Your body is tired, your mind is fading.

Gone

Time flew.
Before I could
hold your hand again,
you were gone for good.

I had planned to visit you,
but never had the time
or so it seemed.
Now you're gone
and I'm
here.

Like leaves fluttering across the pavement,
swirling and darting through invisible currents
with nothing to hold them down –
that's what I pictured when I thought
of you. Your carefree spirit
made me feel alive in ways
I hadn't known I could feel;
in an instant, you vanished
like a child's lost balloon
floating up toward the clouds
and I'm still here.

Cornfields and Bloomers

His brain dried up and he went completely out of his mind,
or at least that's what the doctors said.
His eyes had lost their sparkle, his speech was now
nonexistent.
Before his brain had dried up,
he told the most magnificent stories

about his boyish adventures in the cornfields,
chasing his kid sister's friends with ugly toads
and getting slapped across the knuckles
by an ornery old nun who'd been teaching too long
all because he'd told Janey Sue that her bloomers
were peeking out from under her skirt.

Today he sits in an old oak rocking chair
spending his days staring at pastel birds
on peeling wallpaper.
Today he waits for the Good Lord
to call him home,
where he'll run through the cornfields,
chase his kid sister's friends with ugly toads,
and wonder why he'd ever grown up in the first place.

Obsolete

Weathered pages
outdated,
collecting dust,
occupying space on a coffee table
while people use the internet as a replacement.

Silent Consent

No words are necessary:
a look or touch is all it takes,
signals from the body
read like print on the page.

Present Elsewhere

His rough calloused fingers trace
her dark, wide areola,
the softest part of her tanned breast.
Her body reacts automatically,
but her eyes and mind are elsewhere.

She is far from this place,
not in his company, but the company of another.
She sees her lover's pale, tiny figure
posing on a sandy shore
in a tiny red bikini that serves no real purpose.

Though she pictures her lover,
she still feels his touch;
his coarse hands roam from her breasts
to her legs, spreading them wide
and searching for self-gratifying pleasure.

Freshman

Late September weather brought rain
       and wet tile floors met stumbling feet
              in tennis shoes a size too big.

Step down, down, down in a crowd
       of older students, intimidating to a small
              freshman of fourteen.

Gravity took hold as her white knuckles
       released the handrails, her body curled
              into a ball of blubbering mess

as she struggled to keep my head
       far from the tile floor and other feet
              stepping over her.

Blood rushed to her head,
       cheeks flooded with
              red heat and voices

surrounded her. Arms and hands
       reached for her shriveled body,
              lifting her to wipe the tears.

Twilight

Whoosh, the wind blows;
Croak, the frog knows
      the sounds of the twilight go.
Tap-tap, the tree branch
      on a distant window pane,
Click-clack, clawed paws
        out in the rain,
when suddenly everything falls
    silent.

Sticks and Stones

"Sticks and stones
may break my bones,
but words will never hurt me."
But words will never hurt me -
or will they?

Ugly, fat, disgusting
trash, worthless waste of space.
Stupid, crazy, psycho
bitch with a twisted, gruesome face.

Words hurt more than sticks
and stones when wielded
long enough. Invisible
injuries hurt just as much
as broken bones.

Sticks and stones
will break my bones,
but words will break my mind.
Sticks and stones
may shatter bones,
but words forever remain spoken.

Illusion of a Woman

A woman may be
delicate, fragile, weak -
soft as the petals of a rose.

A woman may be
strong, independent, fierce -
like a lioness on the prowl.

A woman may be
feminine,
masculine,
androgynous -
it matters not.

A woman may be
many things -
every one different, but
beautiful all the same.

A woman may
look like me,
but a woman I am not.

The Art of Something

The art of something isn't hard to master;
so many dreams are filled with the intent
to become something and that something may be a disaster.

Something new every day – the flutter of fingers
on piano keys, the melody not quite heaven sent.
The art of something isn't hard to master.

Practice harder, faster, longer, farther;
new chords and trills and hours spent
in happiness – none of these should bring disaster.

I played my mother's sad song; and look! tears welled
in her eyes as she turned away from my hours spent.
The art of something isn't hard to master.

I learned two new songs, tricky ones. And faster,
this time, I swear, shorter songs but a few less hours spent.
I like them, and it wasn't quite a disaster.

–But no one could compare to you, my darling angel dear
who had countless years and days and hours spent
knowing the art of something you could master
would be beyond compare to my (self-taught) piano
disaster.

Ritual

Ding, the door opens
and swings shut.

Across the grimy floor,
a shuffle of footsteps heaving
a plastic basket overflowing
with the remnants of outfits;
clothing discarded, waiting to take part
in the cleaning ritual once again.
Sorted piles are stuffed
into industrial-sized machines
until it seems too heavy to spin,
hot water and soap make sudsy bubbles.
A fear of bedbugs lingers –
there's no telling who
last used these machines.

Spinning round and round and round,
the mixture of fabrics creates
a hypnotizing kaleidoscope.
Not satisfied with one wash,
another begins with hot water
and detergent with bleach.

Wet garments are moved to another machine
for another hypnotization,
this time tumbling with high heat.
Again not satisfied, a second
tumble in high heat.
Snapping of folding towels,
matching socks, stacks of neatly folded
clothes piled back into the basket.

Ding, the door opens
and swings shut.

Abomination

They say "The heart wants what it wants,"
but my heart is not ordinary.
My heart has room for more than one.

An abomination
they claim I am,
but they lack the ability to understand
that societal norms
are arbitrary
and only seen as acceptable
because society has deemed it so.

They say "You've found your other half,"
and I used to believe that's true
but I am not half of a whole.

I am a whole made of parts on my own
and a partner does not complete me -
but complement and contrast
the parts of me that are mine alone.

The Smoke and the Serpent

Smoke fills the air
and lungs choke
while the serpent slithers,
coiling round and round
the neck of its unsuspecting victim.

No breath can be drawn
even after the smoke clears
because the serpent is ever-present;
when the victim tries
to remove the serpent,
they are unsuccessful.

When the smoke returns
sporadically
the serpent does not release
the grip it holds.

Death is the victim's only
salvation. There is nothing else
that will save them.

Northern Minnesota Armistice

Northern Minnesota rain –
I know it as peace.

Gentle drops pattering on the roof
lull me into a deep sleep.

When it is angry, thunder and lightning
join the rain to put on a concert

for those who reside on the ground below.
Flashes and booms litter the sky

until the clouds clear and the rain fades,
followed by a beautiful arc of colored light.

I long for spring and summer nights
in the northern Minnesota rain.